Rookie
Read-About®
Science

It's a Good Thing There Are
Ladybugs

by Joanne Mattern

Content Consultant

Elizabeth Case DeSantis, M.A. Elementary Education
Julia A. Stark Elementary School, Stamford, Connecticut

Reading Consultant

Jeanne Clidas, Ph.D.
Reading Specialist

Children's Press®
An Imprint of Scholastic Inc.
New York Toronto London Auckland Sydney
Mexico City New Delhi Hong Kong
Danbury, Connecticut

Library of Congress Cataloging-in-Publication Data
Mattern, Joanne, 1963- author.
It's a good thing there are ladybugs/by Joanne Mattern.
     pages cm. — (Rookie read-about science)
Summary: "Introduces the reader to ladybugs and explains the roles they play in the
environment."— Provided by publisher.
Audience: Ages 3-6.
ISBN 978-0-531-22358-1 (library binding: alk. paper) — ISBN 978-0-531-22830-2 (pbk.: alk. paper)
  1. Ladybugs—Juvenile literature. I. Title. II. Title: It is a good thing there are ladybugs. III. Series:
Rookie read-about science.

QL596.C65M29 2015
595.76'9—dc23   2014014970

Produced by Spooky Cheetah Press
Design by Keith Plechaty

© 2015 by Scholastic Inc.

All rights reserved. Published in 2015 by Children's Press, an imprint of Scholastic Inc.

Printed in China 62

SCHOLASTIC, CHILDREN'S PRESS, ROOKIE READ-ABOUT®, and associated logos are trademarks
and/or registered trademarks of Scholastic Inc.

1 2 3 4 5 6 7 8 9 10 R 24 23 22 21 20 19 18 17 16 15

Photographs ©: Alamy Images: 28 center (Flonline digitale Bildagentur GmbH), 28 bottom
(Michael Edward), 12 bottom left (Zoonar GmbH); Christopher Schuster/chris schuster.com: 16;
Dreamstime/Musat Christian: 3 top left, 27 bottom; Media Bakery/B2M Productions: 30 bottom;
Science Source: 12 bottom right (B.G. Thomson), 29 top, 31 top (James H. Robinson), 28 top
(Kenneth M. Highfill), 7, 12 top right, 20 bottom, 23, 27 top left, 31 center top (Nigel Cattlin), 12 top
left (Sheila Terry); Shutterstock, Inc.: 3 bottom (irin-k), cover (Marya Kutuzova); Superstock, Inc.: 3
top right, 15 (age fotostock), 20 top (Biosphoto), 11 (imagebroker.net), 8, 19, 27 top right, 31 bottom
(Juniors), 24, 31 center bottom (NHPA); Thinkstock: 4 (al_louc), 30 top left (Anton Foltin), 30 top
right (PapaBear).

Table of Contents

It's a Good Thing...

Many people like ladybugs because they are pretty. Some people even think they bring good luck. But ladybugs are more than just lucky. It's a good thing there are ladybugs!

A ladybug munches on aphids.

Ladybugs are good friends to farmers and gardeners. That is because ladybugs eat harmful insects called **aphids**. Without ladybugs, aphids would kill a lot of plants.

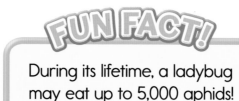

FUN FACT!

During its lifetime, a ladybug may eat up to 5,000 aphids!

Ladybugs are food for other animals, such as frogs, wasps, spiders, and dragonflies.

This unlucky ladybug got caught in a spider's web.

Tiny Insects

A ladybug is an insect that is part of the beetle family. Like other insects, ladybugs have six legs. They have two sets of wings and two **antennas**. Their bodies have three parts: head, thorax, and abdomen.

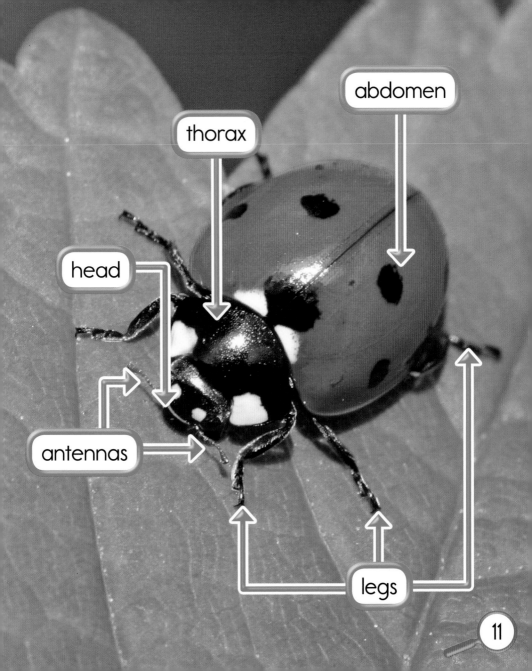

abdomen

thorax

head

antennas

legs

11

harlequin
ladybugs

twenty-two
spot ladybug

two point
ladybug

yellow-shouldered
ladybug

12

All ladybugs are less than ¼-inch (⅔-centimeter) long. They have round or oval bodies.

Ladybugs can have red, orange, yellow, pink, black, or brown shells. Their shells may have spots, stripes, or no markings at all.

FUN FACT!

Ladybugs are also known as ladybird beetles and lady beetles.

Staying Safe

Ladybugs have several ways of protecting themselves. The insect's hard front wings, called the elytra (eh-lih-truh), protect its body from other insects and small **predators**.

elytra

liquid

Ladybugs can also give off a nasty liquid from their legs. Any animal that tries to eat the ladybug will find that it tastes terrible.

The bright markings on the ladybug's shell are for more than decoration. They warn enemies that ladybugs taste bad.

FUN FACT!

The most common ladybug in North America is the seven-spotted ladybug, which has a shiny red-and-black body.

If an animal attacks, the ladybug might play dead. It lies very still until the predator goes away.

A ladybug stays very still until it feels safe.

eggs

larva

A Ladybug's Life

Ladybugs lay eggs on the bottom side of leaves in a garden. The young ladybugs hatch in a few days. They are called larvae. The larvae are very hungry and start eating aphids right away.

FUN FACT!

A female ladybug can lay as many as 2,000 eggs in her lifetime.

The larvae grow quickly. They shed their skin several times before reaching full size. The larva then becomes a pupa. Inside the pupa case, an amazing change is taking place. After two weeks, an adult ladybug comes out.

This shows a ladybug pupa on a leaf.

hese gardeners'
work helping
good thing

After they awake, friends get right to people again. It's there are ladybug

Ladybugs Are Good For...

...protecting plants from harmful insects.

...providing food for animals such as spiders.

...adding beauty to the garden.

As ladybugs age, the color of their spots begins to fade.

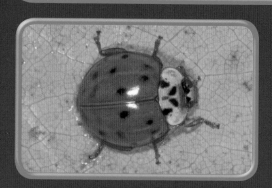

Ladybugs breathe through openings found on the sides of their bodies.

A ladybug can pull its head back into its body.

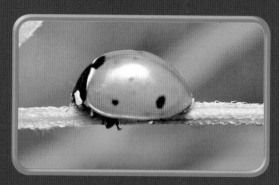

Feature Fun

Most ladybugs are helpful, but some, including the **Mexican bean beetle** and the squash beetle, do eat plants.

RIDDLES

Q. What's the only insect that is not allowed in the boys' bathroom?

A. *A ladybug!*

Q. What is the only thing smaller than a ladybug's mouth?

A. *A ladybug's dinner!*

Creature Feature Fun

Which habitat is right for ladybugs?

A

B

Answer: B. Ladybugs need to live someplace where there are lots of plants and the bugs that eat them.

Plant a Ladybug Garden!

In some places there are not as many ladybugs as there used to be. You can help! Aphids love to munch on rosebushes, and ladybugs love to eat aphids. Ask your parents to plant a rosebush or two in your yard. Then look for ladybugs and enjoy their hard work!

Glossary

antennas (an-TEN-uhs): long, thin feelers on an insect's head

aphids (AY-fids): harmful insects that suck the juices out of plants

hibernate (HYE-bur-nate): spend the winter in a deep sleep

predators (PRED-uh-turs): animals that eat other animals

Index

Facts for Now

Visit this Scholastic Web site for more information on ladybugs:
www.factsfornow.scholastic.com
Enter the keyword **Ladybugs**

About the Author

Joanne Mattern is the author of many books for children. Animals are her favorite subject to write about! She lives in New York State with her husband, four children, and numerous pets, and enjoys finding ladybugs in and around her house.